Introduction

Extreme sports are relatively new sports taken up by daring athletes. They are fun, but can also be dangerous. People who take part in extreme sports must do everything they can to be safe and avoid injuries. BMX racing and freestyle are extreme sports that are growing more and more popular. BMXers ride special bicycles on race courses and jump off **ramps** and **obstacles** to do tricks.

You may have heard of the X Games, held every year in the USA. But do you know what a **half-pipe** is? Do you know the difference between BMX racing and BMX freestyle? Who are the top BMXers in the world today? What do you need to do if you want to take up the sport? This book will answer these and many other questions.

Some BMX riders use a ramp like this one, called a quarter-pipe, to do tricks.

BMX Racing and Freestyle

Julie Nelson

www.raintreepublishers.co.uk
Visit our website to find out more information about **Raintree** books.

To order:
☎ Phone 44 (0) 1865 888112
🖹 Send a fax to 44 (0) 1865 314091
💻 Visit the Raintree Bookshop at www.raintreepublishers.co.uk to browse our catalogue and order online.

First published in Great Britain by Raintree Publishers, Halley Court, Jordan Hill, Oxford, OX2 8EJ, part of Harcourt Education.
Raintree is a registered trademark of Harcourt Education Ltd.

Consultants: Dan Quigley, Penn Cycle; Jerry Landrum, BMX Mania

Editor: Isabel Thomas
Cover design: Michelle Lisseter
Production: Jonathan Smith

Originated by Dot Gradations Ltd
Printed and bound in China and Hong Kong by South China

ISBN 1 844 21291 2
07 06 05 04 03
10 9 8 7 6 5 4 3 2 1

British Library Cataloguing in Publication Data
A catalogue for this book is available from the British Library

Acknowledgements
The publishers would like to thank the following for permission to reproduce photographs: Tony Donaldson: pp. **1, 4, 8-9, 12, 14, 18–19, 22, 24, 26–27, 29, 30, 32, 34, 36, 40, 42 top, 42 bottom, 43 top, 43 bottom**; Unicorn/Jeff Greenberg: pp. **10, 17**; Unicorn/Les Van: p. **6**

Cover photograph reproduced with permission of Action Plus.

Every effort has been made to contact copyright holders of any material reproduced in this book. Any omissions will be rectified in subsequent printings if notice is given to the publishers.

Contents

BMX freestylers use their bikes to do tricks.

How to use this book

This book is divided into parts called chapters. The title of each chapter tells you what it is about. A list of chapters and their page numbers appears in the table of contents on page 3. The index on page 48 gives you page numbers where you can find the main topics discussed in this book.

Each chapter has colourful photographs, captions and boxes. The photographs show you some of the things written about in the book, so you will know what they look like. A caption is an explanation that tells you about a photograph. The captions in this book are in pale blue boxes. Special boxes give you extra information about the subject.

You may not know what some of the words in this book mean. To learn new words, you should look them up in a dictionary. This book has a small dictionary called a glossary. Words that appear in **bold** type are explained in the glossary on page 44.

You can use the Internet sites listed on page 46 to learn more about topics discussed in this book. You can write letters to the addresses listed on page 46, asking them questions or asking them to send you helpful information.

BMX racing and freestyle

BMX stands for bicycle motocross. A BMX race is a bicycle race on a dirt track. The track contains many sharp turns, hills and bumps.

BMX racers have to ride in mud and dirt. They ride standing up on their bikes. Sometimes there are crashes or **wipeouts**.

This BMX rider has used a ramp to turn upside down at a competition.

Early BMX riders tried to imitate motorcycle riders on their bikes.

Freestyle

Another type of BMX bicycle riding is called freestyle. Freestyle riders do tricks with their bikes. They do not compete in races. Judges give them points for being good at tricks. They also get points for doing tricks that are original and difficult. In freestyle, the rider with the most points wins.

How BMX and freestyle began

BMX racing began in the early 1970s in California, USA. Some young bike riders had the idea of using their bicycles to imitate motocross riders. Motocross is a type of motorcycle dirt racing. Soon, manufacturers were making bikes specially designed for 'off-road' riding. Then groups of riders got together on rough ground to practise their new skills. These groups soon became organized clubs. A new sport was born.

Freestyle also started in the 1970s in California. Some young people had the idea of doing skateboarding tricks with their bicycles. Another new sport was born.

It didn't take long before this exciting sport spread around the world. BMX arrived in countries such as Great Britain and Australia. In the early 1980s it became an internationally recognized sport.

All BMX riders will crash at some time. That is why they wear helmets and protective equipment and clothing.

Getting organized

By 1981, the International BMX Federation had begun to organize BMX racing around the world. In 1982, the first BMX championships were held in Daytona, Florida, in the USA. Today, BMX and freestyle are more popular than ever.

BMX races and freestyle competitions take place all around the world. They are especially popular in the USA and Europe, where people of all ages compete. Rules and regulations are based on the international rules set by the International Cycling Union or Union Cycliste Internationale (UCI).

BMX events are held all year round. Each race starts with the riders standing on their bikes in a **starting gate**. The riders try to be the fastest out of the gate at the start of the race.

The leader of a race may use any part of the track. The other racers must get around the leader without crashing. Riders are allowed to touch each other, but they cannot crash on purpose. Riders who try dangerous things can be disqualified or placed in last position at the end of the race.

A BMX race is made up of three races called **motos**. One moto can take from thirty seconds to one minute to finish, and is one lap of the track. A moto is made up of as few as two riders and no more than eight riders at a time.

 This is the BMX track at the X Games.

Points and classes

Each rider is given points for the place where he or she finishes. The top racer gets one point. Riders who finish further back get more points. At the end of the three qualifying motos, the riders with the least points race in a moto called a **main**. After the main, the rider with the least points is the champion.

There are many classes of BMX race. Riders are put into different groups based on age and skill level. The most experienced riders race each other. New riders are placed into their own motos.

BMX tracks

A BMX race track can be inside or outside. Indoor tracks are good when the weather is bad. They also allow races to take place after dark. Indoor tracks are usually shorter than outdoor tracks and the races are quicker.

BMX dirt tracks are made of mud, sand and gravel. They are 7 to 8 metres wide at the start. Some tracks are less than 3 metres wide in places.

Each race begins at a gate on top of a hill. The gate opens or drops to start the race. Riders must stay in their own lane for the first 15 metres. After that, they are free to choose their own route around the track.

Tracks contain many obstacles. These are difficult places to ride and they include hills, bumps, jumps, water and sharp turns. Water and mud jumps are called hazards. Racers aim to jump and land smoothly so they don't loose any speed. Some try to jump as high as possible and others do tricks in the air.

Some hazards

There are many types of bump and hill. High jumps can cause big crashes. **Whoop-de-doos**, or rhythm sections, are a series of several small hills. Riding over them is like riding on a roller coaster.

Tracks also have difficult turns. A **berm** is a fast turn with a high bank on the inside of the turn. A flat turn has no bank. Riders can fall more easily on flat turns. An **esse** is a turn that goes to the right and then to the left, like the letter S.

The end of the race is called the **final stretch** or the last straightaway. It is usually a short distance of straight, flat track. The bikers race as fast as they can up the final stretch to see who wins.

What is freestyle like?

There are freestyle competitions for one person, for two people riding together and for teams of riders. Freestyle bikers can do ground tricks on flat surfaces called flatland. They also use road kerbs or curved ramps to do jumps and other tricks.

Freestyle riders do many tricks using ramps. Most ramps are made of concrete or wood and are curved. They look like pipes that have been cut in half or in quarters. They are called half-pipes and **quarter-pipes**.

This BMX freestyler is doing an aerial.

Riders ride up the ramp curves to do jumps called **aerials**. They ride off the edge of the ramps and do turns and flips in the air. Then they land again on the ramp. A quarter-pipe is the most common BMX ramp. It is used to get the bike and rider up to 8 metres above the ground. Beginners use mini-ramps to practise tricks before they try the real thing. Today, freestyle is even more popular than BMX racing.

Getting started

Safety is an important part of becoming a good rider. Riders must wear safe equipment and clothing. They must protect their bodies. Riders can fall or crash at any time.

Helmets are the most important pieces of safety equipment. They stop the head from being injured if the rider crashes. Helmets also protect the ears and face. Most helmets have a visor that shields eyes from the sun. Riders should also wear mouth guards that are either built into their helmets or strapped onto them.

These riders at the X Games are wearing helmets to protect their heads.

Staying safe

Safe riders wear long trousers and a long-sleeved shirt. They wear trousers that will not get stuck in the bike spokes. They always wear shoes and socks when biking.

Safe riders always wear safety equipment. This includes a helmet, gloves, knee pads and elbow pads.

If they fall, safe riders roll away from their bikes. They try to keep their arms and legs close to their bodies. They do this to avoid getting run over by other riders.

Safe riders take good care of their bikes. They check before every race to see that all the parts are working properly.

Safe riders never give other people a ride on their bikes.

Safe riders do not race or try tricks in the street. They do these things only at a track or in an area away from traffic.

Safe riders practise tricks and race skills only when other people are around, in case a rider gets injured. An injury is some kind of hurt or damage, such as a broken bone or a sprain. A sprain means one of the body's joints has been twisted, tearing its muscles or ligaments. A ligament holds together the bones in a joint.

Safety equipment

Several other parts of a rider's body should also be protected. Elbows and knees can get bumped and scraped. Padded BMX clothes called leathers protect riders. Extra pads for their knees and elbows are also available.

Riders should cover as much of their skin as possible. They should always wear long-sleeved shirts and long trousers. They should also wear gloves. Leather gloves help riders grip their bike handles better. They also protect their hands during a crash.

It is important that riders tuck in the bottom of their trouser legs. If trousers are not secured, they can catch in the sprockets or spokes of a bike. Socks and shoes should always be worn. The shoes a rider wears should have good grip on the bottoms.

Rider profile: Jill Kintner

Jill Kintner has won many BMX titles in the USA. Her favourite win was in the Junior Women's class at the World Championships. Kintner is one of today's top pros and has advice for young people who want to ride. 'Ride as much as you can, all the time,' she says. 'It's the best way to learn.'

This freestyle bike was made especially for doing tricks.

The bikes

Early racers used their ordinary bikes to race. They fixed them up so they would race better. This was called 'souping up' the bikes. Riders changed the bikes to make them stronger for racing. They wore helmets and home-made padding to protect their bodies. Young people made their own dirt tracks on waste land and in fields.

Modern BMX bikes are different to road bikes. They are stronger and designed to be easy to ride and steer. They weigh less. Most BMX bikes weigh just 8 to 13.5 kilograms. They have different kinds of tyres and other parts to a normal bike. BMX tyres have knobs on them to help grip the ground. The wheels are small, but filled with lots of air.

BMX bikes are sometimes padded to protect the rider. The padding is soft so that the rider does not get injured easily in a crash.

Freestylers use different kinds of bikes to BMX racers. A freestyle bike must be strong and light to make it easier to do tricks. Metal plates called gussets can be welded to the frame to make the bike stronger, without adding too much extra weight.

This BMX racer is turning on a berm.

Freestyle bikes

Freestyle bikes have handlebars and seats that can twist to help riders do tricks. The part that allows the handlebars to twist is called a rotor. There are also steps called platforms on the wheels, handlebars and pedals. Riders stand on these platforms when they do tricks. Freestyle bikes also have smoother tyres than racing bikes. They all have brakes on the handlebars, and a few have brakes on the pedals as well. BMX racing bikes use only hand brakes.

BMX timeline

Early 1970s: Young people begin imitating motocross

1976: Freestyle begins

1981: International BMX Federation starts

1982: First BMX World Championships are held

1993: BMX is fully integrated into the UCI

Becoming a BMX
racer or freestyle rider

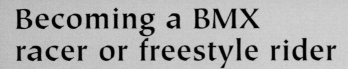

Almost anyone can become a BMX or freestyle rider if he or she is in good physical shape. Riders must have strong legs and healthy lungs.

Beginners must practise for a long time before they can do tricks like this.

They can start when they are as young as three or four. World champion Jill Kintner began riding at age eight.

BMX racers study the track before a race. They learn all the obstacles and think about how to ride different parts of the race. Many riders walk around the race track before a race. Every track is different.

The start is a big part of the race. Some say it is the hardest part. It is important because the rider who gets the best start has the lead. The leader can use any part of the track to keep the lead.

Racing skills

Getting the **holeshot** means taking the lead out of the starting gate. The best way to win the holeshot is to work on timing at the gate. Riders try to move before the gate even opens, leaving just as it drops.

Riders sometimes use their feet and legs to push against the ground on sharp turns. Some experienced riders put out a foot to block other bikes from passing them. This can be dangerous though, and should only be done by experienced riders.

Good riders can hit berms at high speeds. They learn how not to slow down. Riders who do not slow down in flat turns, however, can **wipeout**.

One place riders try to get around the leader is on the berms. This is called 'berm warfare'.

Rider profile: Greg Hill

Greg Hill is one of the best-known riders in BMX history. He started racing in 1977. He won all his races at the age of fourteen and then turned pro. He was injured many times, but he always worked hard to come back. Many people think he is one of the best racers ever. He now speaks to groups about his racing career.

These BMX racers have just left the
starting gate.

Flying high over big jumps looks daring. Riders
often crash when they land big jumps. Those who do
not crash usually land on the back wheel first. If a
rider lands on the front wheel first or on both wheels
at the same time, they will probably crash.

Riders learn how to fall in the right way to avoid
injury. This involves pushing the bike away from their
body and falling onto their kneepads first.

This is Dave Mirra doing a no-footer back flip to earn points from a judge at the X Games.

Smart riders

Clever riders try not to fly too high on jumps. They lose too much time when they do. The race is not about who jumps highest, but is about who finishes the race fastest.

Riding freestyle

Freestyle riding is often about who can land the highest jumps and do the best tricks. In the kind of freestyle called mini, or street, riders use benches, kerbs, walls and handrails to do tricks. These obstacles are found on or near roads. Sometimes small ramps are also used for tricks and jumps.

Flatriding freestyle is done without ramps or obstacles. Riders do different kinds of tricks, including spins and twirls.

Vert riding is a high-flying form of freestyle. Riders use half-pipe and quarter-pipe ramps to catch **big air**. This allows them to do more difficult tricks. Another high-flying form of freestyle riding is called dirt jumping. Dirt jumpers use dirt obstacles and ramps to catch air and do tricks.

This kind of aerial trick is attempted only by experienced riders.

Learning freestyle skills

The best way to learn freestyle tricks is to practise with another rider. One person can hold the bike while the other person practises. This way tricks can also be done with less chance of falling.

Freestyle riders should not try to do too many things at once. They should first learn ground tricks, such as **wheelies**. A wheelie is done by riding the bike with the front wheel off the ground. Another ground trick is a **kick turn**. A kick turn is done on a hill. The rider gets to the top of the hill and stops with the front wheel in the air. Then the rider twists the bike around to where it started and rides back down the hill.

Other ground tricks are **pogoing, sidewalking** and **endos**. Pogoing is done by hopping on one tyre. Sidewalking is done by hopping sideways. Endos are done by balancing a bike on only the front tyre. If a rider falls over the front of the bike, that is also called an endo.

After learning ground tricks, riders can learn ramp tricks. Aerials are ramp tricks done on a bike in mid air. The ramp is used to get the bike and rider off the ground.

Aerials

There are many kinds of aerial trick. In a **kick out**, the rider throws the bike to the side in midair. In a **tabletop jump**, the rider lays the bike out flat in the air. Riders can also do aerial turns and endos.

Where to train

BMX racers and freestylers can practise at many places. Many towns have BMX tracks. Official tracks can be used for training, practise or competition. Official tracks are approved by BMX organizations. There are also BMX clubs people can join. The clubs **sponsor** races. Clubs also give information about other races around the country and the world.

Riders do not need a full track to train. They can use empty car parks, empty pieces of land, woods or open fields. Freestylers can practise at BMX tracks and at skateboard parks. They can also make their own ramps at home out of wood. They can try tricks on hills they find near driveways or on empty land. Some freestylers even practise in empty swimming pools. Young riders should always practise with an adult watching.

It is important not to practise on streets or around cars. This can be dangerous. Riders and freestylers should always wear safety gear, even when practising. It is safer to practise with other people around, in case somebody gets injured.

These riders are experienced at riding whoop-de-doos.

Who are the professional riders?

Professional BMX and freestyle riders get paid to race, just like professional football players get paid to play football. A professional, or pro, is a person who gets paid to do what many people do just for fun. Riders must decide if they are good enough to turn pro. A rider who always wins all of his or her races might be ready to turn pro.

Professionals take good care of themselves and their bikes. They must train hard. They need to be in very good physical shape to race. They need strong legs and lungs. They cannot get tired in the middle of races.

Sponsors

A sponsor is a business or a person who pays for a rider or team to race. The sponsor pays for the bikes and also for safety equipment. Some sponsors pay for riders to travel to races around the country and the world.

Many sponsors are bike companies or shoe companies. Riders wear each sponsor's name on their leathers and on their bikes. Sponsors hope people will see their names and remember them.

Most riders never get sponsors. You do not need a sponsor to race. Only the top experts ever find sponsors who help them with expenses.

Rider profile: David Mirra

Dave Mirra has won more X Games BMX medals than anyone else. Ten of his medals are gold and three are silver. He started racing in 1981 and turned pro in 1987. His nickname is 'Miracle Boy'. He has won a medal in almost every event he's been in since 1995. He is famous for a double flip he did at one X Games.

Competing in BMX racing and freestyle

Hundreds of thousands of people ride in BMX races and freestyle events. BMX riders can start at an early age. More people see BMX racing on TV and in person than ever before. They also read about BMX in books and magazines.

The sport of BMX has changed a lot since it began. The bikes are lighter and faster. The safety equipment is better. The tracks are more difficult but more fun to ride on. BMX races are now held all over the world.

Did you know?

Did you know that some BMX riders and fans have special ways of saying things? When they say 'wired', they mean to do a trick right. When they say 'amped', they mean to be excited. They call a helmet a 'brain bucket' or a 'lid'. A rider who gets very dirty is called a 'corndog'. A wheel that gets bent badly is called a 'potato chip'.

Millions of people have watched Dave Mirra
on television in X Games BMX competitions.

X Games and popularity

One of the most famous BMX events is called the X Games. These were begun by the USA sports television station ESPN in 1995 and were known as the Extreme Games. Today, this competition has become the best-known competition for all kinds of extreme sport.

Some people who make money from racing carry on racing when they are in their thirties and forties. They study the tracks they race. They learn which bikes are the best. They take good care of themselves and their equipment. It is the combined effort of people of all ages that makes BMX such a popular sport.

Rider profile: Mat Hoffman

Mat Hoffman is known as 'The Condor'. He began racing in 1982 and turned pro two years later. In 2000, he came back from being injured. That year he finished first or second in every event he entered and third in the X Games. Hoffman helped make freestyling well known to the world. He was the world champion from 1987 to 1996. He has his own business called Hoffman Bikes.

Quick facts about
BMX sports

- There were more than 60,000 members of the American Bicycle Association in 2000.

- In the 1996 X-Games, Mat Hoffman won the gold medal for freestyle. He did it with three broken bones in his foot.

- One of the most famous bike companies is Redline. It started in 1972, and all its bikes are red and black.

- Freestyler Bob Haro did some of his freestyle tricks as a stuntman in the film *ET: The Extra-Terrestrial*.

- Outside the USA, BMX racing and freestyle are most popular in Australia and Europe.

- The BMX world record for the 45.5-metre (50-yard) dash is held by Brian Lopes, who raced that distance in 4.78 seconds.

- A wallride is a difficult trick that involves riding along a vertical wall for a few seconds before jumping back onto a ramp.

Glossary

aerial trick done in midair with the help of a ramp

berm banked turn

big air when a rider jumps as high as they can into the
   air off a ramp to do tricks

endo balancing the bike on only the front tyre; *also*
   when a rider falls over the front of their bike

esse turn on the track that curves both ways, like the
   letter S

final stretch straight run at the end of a race

half-pipe U-shaped ramp with two curved walls

helmet hard kind of hat that protects a person's head

holeshot to grab an early lead out of the gate

kick out trick where the rider throws the bike to the
   side in midair

kick turn trick where the rider turns around at the top
   of the ramp

main final race of an event to determine the champion

moto one lap or one race on a track

obstacle something that makes a track more
    difficult to ride

pogoing hopping on one tyre

professional person who makes money doing something
    amateurs do for fun

quarter-pipe curved ramp used to get high for aerials

ramp curved surface used for freestyle tricks

sidewalking hopping sideways on a bike

sponsor company who pays someone to use or advertise
    its product

starting gate area at the front of the race where
    riders begin

tabletop jump trick where the rider lays the bike flat in
    the air

wheelie riding on only the back tyre

whoop-de-doos many bumps close together on a track

wipeout when a rider falls off their bike

Internet sites and addresses

British Cycling Federation

www.bcf.uk.com

BMX Southwest Region

www.bmxsouthwest.com

BMX Australia Inc.

Ground Floor, 120 Jolimont Road
Jolimont 3002, PO Box 1026
North Richmond, Victoria 3121

BMX Australia Community

bmxa.actbmx.com.au/bmx

UCI BMX

www.uci.ch/english/bmx

EXPN.Com BMX Index

expn.go.com/bmx

Books and magazines

Extreme sports: BMX Biking, Dick, Scott. Heinemann
   Library, Oxford, 2002

Extreme sports: BMX, Job, Chris. Raintree Publishers,
   Oxford, 2003

Ride BMX Magazine (UK)
   This magazine looks at BMX racing and freestyle in
   the UK. There are nine issues every year, with news
   about competitions, people and equipment.

Dig BMX Magazine
   This magazine comes out every fortnight, with news
   about BMX in Europe and the USA. See their website
   www.digbmx.com for more information.

Fat Magazine (www.fatbmx.com)
   This is an online magazine, with BMX news and
   gossip from around the world.

Index